Success With

Grammar

SCHOLASTIC

Editor: Ourania Papacharalambous
Cover design by Tannaz Fassihi; cover illustration by Kevin Zimmer
Interior design by Cynthia Ng
Interior Illustrations by Rusty Fletcher (3, 12, 18, 45); Doug Jones (6, 9, 14, 21, 30, 32, 41, 42, 44)

ISBN 978-1-338-79843-2
Scholastic Inc., 557 Broadway, New York, NY 10012
Copyright © 2022 Scholastic Inc.
All rights reserved. Printed in the U.S.A.
First printing, January 2022
1 2 3 4 5 6 7 8 9 10   40   29 28 27 26 25 24 23 22

INTRODUCTION

No other resource boosts grammar skills like *Scholastic Success With Grammar*! For classroom or at-home use, this exciting series for grades 1 through 5 provides invaluable reinforcement and practice in grammar topics such as sentence types, verb tenses, parts of speech, subject-verb agreement, common and proper nouns, punctuation, sentence structure, capitalization, and more!

This 48-page book contains loads of clever practice pages to keep kids challenged and excited as they strengthen the grammar skills they need to read and write well. Each practice page reinforces a specific, age-appropriate skill. On page 4, you will find a list of the key skills covered in the activities throughout this book. What's more, the activities for each skill are followed by an assessment sheet that gives students realistic practice in taking tests—and gives you a useful tool to follow their progress!

Take the lead and help students succeed with *Scholastic Success With Grammar*. Parents and teachers agree: No one helps students succeed like Scholastic!

TABLE OF CONTENTS

Grade-Appropriate Skills Covered in Scholastic Success With Grammar: Grade 5

Know and apply grade-level phonics and word analysis skills in decoding words.

Read with sufficient accuracy and fluency to support comprehension.

Demonstrate command of the conventions of standard English grammar and usage when writing or speaking.

Form and use the perfect verb tenses.

Use verb tense to convey various times, sequences, states, and conditions.

Recognize and correct inappropriate shifts in verb tense.

Write informative/explanatory texts to examine a topic and convey ideas and information clearly.

Introduce a topic clearly, provide a general observation and focus, and group related information logically; include formatting, illustrations, and multimedia when useful to aiding comprehension.

Develop the topic with facts, definitions, concrete details, quotations, or other information and examples related to the topic.

Link ideas within and across categories of information using words, phrases, and clauses.

Use precise language and domain-specific vocabulary to inform about or explain the topic.

Provide a concluding statement or section related to the information or explanation presented.

Demonstrate command of the conventions of standard English capitalization, punctuation, and spelling when writing.

Use punctuation to separate items in a series.

Use a comma to separate an introductory element from the rest of the sentence.

Spell grade-appropriate words correctly, consulting references as needed.

Use knowledge of language and its conventions when writing, speaking, reading, or listening.

Expand, combine, and reduce sentences for meaning, reader/listener interest, and style.

Complete and Simple Subjects

Circle the complete subject in each sentence.

1 This story tells about Jamie and Gramma Bowman.

2 Gramma Bowman used to tell Jamie stories.

3 Jamie's great-grandmother loved to see the fox's tracks.

4 Her best friend, Pippin the Fox, left the tracks.

5 That clever fox delighted Gramma.

6 Gramma's song is a kind of fox song.

Underline the complete subject once and the simple subject twice.

1 The autumn leaves were blowing in the wind.

2 The old man told a story about the leaves.

3 The fall season is the time for leaf dances.

4 The leaves put on their best colors at that time.

5 The cold, autumn wind comes to take them.

6 Gramma Bowman, a wise woman, told Jamie this.

7 The old leaves are like old people.

8 Their final dances are very beautiful.

9 The very best dances occur in autumn.

10 Gramma Bowman's story explains a natural event.

Complete and Simple Subjects

Read the sentences below. Underline each complete subject once.

1. Old, wise Gramma Bowman teaches Jamie a song.

2. The first line of the song is "Hey, kwah nu deh."

3. The words of the song repeat.

4. This song, a kind of chant, stays in Jamie's memory forever.

5. Her dream includes this song.

6. A fox with glistening eyes appears in the answer to the song.

7. The fox, a mysterious animal, disappears again.

Read the sentences below. Underline each simple subject twice.

1. The events in Jamie's dream tell a great deal.

2. Her conversations in the dream show her relationship to Gramma Bowman.

3. Their actions reveal a loving closeness.

4. Jamie, Gramma Bowman's great granddaughter, learns from her.

5. Both characters enjoy each other's company.

6. Gramma's lessons to her will live on in Jamie's memory.

7. Gramma Bowman, a guide and teacher, shares her knowledge.

8. The world of nature is Gramma's home.

Complete and Simple Subjects

Fill in the bubble next to the complete subject of each sentence.

1 Jamie's great-grandmother was from Spain.
○ Jamie's great-grandmother
○ Spain
○ great-grandmother

2 This amazing woman moved in with Jamie's family.
○ woman
○ amazing woman
○ This amazing woman

3 Their house on the Winooski River had a maple woods behind it.
○ Winooski River
○ Their house on the Winooski River
○ had a maple woods

4 The woods up the hill contained birch trees.
○ The woods
○ contained birch trees
○ The woods up the hill

5 Sweet, wild blueberries grew there.
○ blueberries
○ Sweet, wild blueberries
○ wild blueberries

Fill in the bubble next to the simple subject of each sentence.

1 Early settlers from France moved to the area.
○ settlers
○ France
○ Early settlers from France

2 Blueberries were plentiful in the summer.
○ Blueberries
○ summer
○ plentiful

3 The dead blueberry bushes are burned each fall.
○ blueberry
○ are burned
○ bushes

4 The new, green plants will be stronger in the spring.
○ green plants
○ plants
○ spring

5 Proper care of plants makes a difference.
○ care
○ makes
○ plants

Complete and Simple Predicates

Underline the complete predicate once and the simple predicate twice. Then, write *A* if the simple predicate is an action verb, or *B* if it is a state-of-being verb.

> The **complete predicate** is all the words in the predicate of a sentence. The **simple predicate** is the main word in the complete predicate. It is the verb, the word that shows action or state of being.

1 My classmates and I often listen to the radio. _____

2 We like the latest pop music. _____

3 Our class danced in the gym last Friday afternoon. _____

4 Some of the teachers at the dance sang some "oldies." _____

5 The dance was a huge success among students and teachers. _____

6 Some parents stood along the side of the gym. _____

7 They seemed amused by the music and dancing. _____

. . . .

For each complete subject, write a complete predicate. Then, underline the complete predicate once and the simple predicate twice. Use action verbs and state-of-being verbs.

1 My fifth-grade class _____

_____

2 Some of the younger students in my school _____

_____

3 My favorite book _____

_____

4 The movie _____

_____

Complete and Simple Predicates

Read the sentences below.
Underline each complete predicate once.

1. The game against the Kansas City Royals would start soon.

2. The left fielder was running out to the field beside Ken.

3. A tingle of excitement ran down Ken Jr.'s back.

4. The new left fielder was none other than his dad.

5. The crowd at the stadium let out a roar.

6. All the fans, in the stadium and out of it, knew this was a great moment.

7. Ken, the left fielder's son, felt so happy!

Read the sentences below. Underline each simple predicate twice.

1. I read the story of Ken Griffey Jr. and Sr.

2. These two famous players are father and son.

3. They even played on the same team together.

4. Both men were in the Seattle Mariners line-up.

5. This father-son team made history.

6. The president of the United States sent them a telegram after one great game.

7. The Griffeys appeared together on a few television shows.

8. These two great athletes remain famous today.

Complete and Simple Predicates

Read each sentence. Fill in the bubble next to the complete predicate.

1 Our fifth-grade class performed a musical Friday.
- ○ fifth-grade class
- ○ performed a musical Friday
- ○ performed

2 Parents and teachers attended the event, too.
- ○ attended the event, too
- ○ attended
- ○ Parents and teachers

3 Mr. Stein, our teacher, was the musical director.
- ○ Mr. Stein, our teacher
- ○ was the musical director
- ○ the musical director

4 He also chose the musical numbers.
- ○ He also chose
- ○ chose
- ○ chose the musical numbers

5 Some of us worked behind the scenes.
- ○ worked behind the scenes
- ○ Some of us
- ○ worked

Read each sentence. Fill in the bubble next to the simple predicate.

1 Some students were in charge of building the stage sets.
- ○ Some students
- ○ were
- ○ in charge of

2 Others collected costumes.
- ○ collected
- ○ collected costumes
- ○ Others

3 Any kind of performance is definitely a group effort!
- ○ performance
- ○ is definitely
- ○ is

4 Everyone was a little nervous before the performance.
- ○ was
- ○ Everyone
- ○ nervous

5 Mr. Stein congratulated us after the thunderous applause.
- ○ thunderous applause
- ○ Mr. Stein
- ○ congratulated

Compound Subjects and Predicates

A **compound subject** is two or more simple subjects joined by the **conjunction** *and* or *or*.

A **compound predicate** is two or more simple predicates joined by the **conjunction** *and* or *or*.

If the sentence has a compound subject, underline each simple subject once. Circle the conjunction. If the sentence has a compound predicate, underline each verb twice. Circle the conjunction.

1 Families and friends often help each other during times of hardship.

2 During a war, people sometimes leave their homes and lose their belongings.

3 Intelligence, courage, and luck can help people survive.

4 Food and clean water may become scarce.

5 Many young people join the army or work in factories.

. . . .

Read each pair of sentences. Then, combine them to form a compound subject or a compound predicate. Write your new sentence on the line.

1 Annemarie played with the dolls. Ellen played with the dolls.

_____

2 Kirsti cried about the shoes. Kirsti complained about the shoes.

_____

3 Annemarie brushed her hair. Annemarie handed the brush to Ellen.

_____

4 Families hid in the house. Families fled to the forest.

_____

Compound Subjects and Predicates

Read the sentences. Underline compound subjects once and compound predicates twice. Circle the conjunctions.

1 Annemarie and Ellen are good friends.

2 Their homes and families are in Denmark.

3 The girls sometimes talk or giggle with Annemarie's sister.

4 All three children joke, laugh, and play games together.

5 The Rosens or the Johansens will be there.

6 Families and friends help each other in time of war.

7 The Johansens hide Ellen and keep her safe.

8 Ellen reads and sings to Kirsti.

9 Denmark, Holland, and other countries struggled during the war.

10 People succeed or fail in surprising ways.

- -

Select two sentences from above, one with a compound subject and one with a compound predicate. Rewrite each sentence with your own compound subject or predicate.

1 _____

_____

2 _____

_____

Compound Subjects and Predicates

Decide if the underlined part of each sentence is correct.
Fill in the bubble next to the correct answer.

1 <u>I, George, and Tina</u> are playground monitors.
- ○ George and I and Tina
- ○ George, Tina, and I
- ○ correct as is

2 We <u>watch for problems and solve</u> them.
- ○ watch solve for problems,
- ○ watch for problems or solve.
- ○ correct as is

3 <u>Keith and Tracy</u> asked me for help with a problem.
- ○ Keith, and Tracy
- ○ Keith, Tracy
- ○ correct as is

4 Their friend Matt <u>hit a ball lost it</u> on the school roof.
- ○ hit a ball, lost it
- ○ hit a ball and lost it
- ○ correct as is

5 <u>I and Tina</u> found Matt in a corner of the playground.
- ○ Tina and I
- ○ I or Tina
- ○ correct as is

6 He <u>pointed showed us</u> where it went.
- ○ pointed and showed us
- ○ pointed or showed us
- ○ correct as is

7 Tina <u>looked up, turned, walked</u> over to Ms. Weiss.
- ○ looked up, turned, and walked
- ○ looked up and turned, walked
- ○ correct as is

8 Ms. Weiss <u>joined us or helped</u> with the discussion.
- ○ joined us and helped
- ○ joined us, helped
- ○ correct as is

9 Ms. Weiss said we could <u>get the custodian, find</u> another ball.
- ○ get the custodian, and find
- ○ get the custodian or find
- ○ correct as is

10 Matt <u>smiled and went to find</u> the custodian.
- ○ smiled, and went to find
- ○ smiled and, went to find
- ○ correct as is

Compound Sentences

A compound sentence is a sentence made up of two simple sentences joined by a comma and the conjunction *and*, *but*, or *or*.

Circle the conjunction in parentheses ( ) that makes sense. Then, rewrite the sentence using the conjunction.

1 I want to go to the movies, _____ my friend Pat does not. (or, but)

_____

2 It rained last night, _____ we had to stay home. (and, but)

_____

3 Ed will drive to Texas, _____ he will take the train. (or, and)

_____

4 It snowed this morning, _____ the sun came out this afternoon. (but, or)

_____

Write a compound sentence from the two simple sentences. Use the conjunction shown in parentheses ( ).

1 We wanted to ride our bikes home. Mine had a flat tire. (but)

_____

2 I will finish the job today. Bob will finish it tomorrow. (or)

_____

3 The whistle blew. The train pulled out of the station. (and)

_____

Compound Sentences

In the space provided, combine each pair of sentences into one compound sentence. Use a comma and choose the conjunction *(and, but,* or *or)* that makes the most sense.

1 Our cousins arrived. We were very happy to see them.

_____

2 Eileen had cut her hair short. Her twin sister, Emily, still had long hair.

_____

3 They had always looked exactly alike. I could not get used to them!

_____

4 Would they play with me? Would they only play with my older sisters?

_____

5 First, Eileen gave me a hug. Then, Emily did the same.

_____

· ·

Write a paragraph about a skill or sport you have learned. Use different types of sentences to make your writing interesting.

_____

_____

_____

_____

_____

_____

Compound Sentences

Decide if there is an error in the underlined part of each compound sentence. Fill in the bubble next to the correct answer.

1 We cleaned our house last <u>weekend and I</u> threw out some old books and toys.
- ○ weekend but I
- ○ weekend, and I
- ○ correct as is

2 Old toys went in a big plastic <u>bag, but old books</u> went in a box.
- ○ bag, old books
- ○ bag or old books
- ○ correct as is

3 I could have cleared my <u>bookshelf, and</u> I wanted to keep a few old favorites.
- ○ bookshelf, but I
- ○ bookshelf, And I
- ○ correct as is

4 I gave some toys to a <u>neighbor but, most</u> went to the thrift store.
- ○ neighbor, but most
- ○ neighbor and most
- ○ correct as is

5 We drove to the thrift <u>store, and I</u> helped carry the boxes inside.
- ○ store and I
- ○ store, But I
- ○ correct as is

6 I wanted to look around the <u>store but we</u> didn't have time.
- ○ store and we
- ○ store, but we
- ○ correct as is

7 I saw an old typewriter <u>there, and no one</u> uses those things anymore!
- ○ there, but no one
- ○ there but No one
- ○ correct as is

8 We stopped at the <u>library, and each</u> of us checked out some books.
- ○ library, Each
- ○ library and each
- ○ correct as is

9 My shelves looked <u>empty, the library books</u> helped fill them up a little.
- ○ empty, but the library books
- ○ empty, or the library books
- ○ correct as is

10 I love my old <u>books but, my interests</u> have changed as I've gotten older.
- ○ books but my interests
- ○ books, but my interests
- ○ correct as is

Common and Proper Nouns

Read the sentences below. Underline any common nouns in each sentence once and any proper nouns twice.

> A **common noun** names any person, place, animal, or thing. A **proper noun** names a specific person, place, animal, or thing and begins with a capital letter.

1 Mr. Sherlock Holmes is a famous fictional detective.

2 This character was created by Sir Arthur Conan Doyle.

3 Holmes appeared in 56 stories and several novels written by Doyle, including *The Sign of Four.*

4 He was often assisted by his friend Dr. John Watson.

5 They worked together on mysteries throughout the city of London.

Read the sentences below. Identify the underlined words in each sentence as proper or common nouns.

1 <u>Peter Jones</u> is a <u>detective</u> who works at <u>Scotland Yard</u>.

_____

2 Yesterday, <u>Mr. Reginald Merryweather</u> came to him with a very strange <u>story</u>.

_____

3 It seems that rare <u>coins</u> are missing from the <u>Bank of London</u> where he works.

_____

4 The <u>money</u> was kept in a <u>safe</u> at the <u>bank</u>.

_____

5 <u>Peter Jones</u> decided to call <u>Sherlock Holmes</u> to assist him with the <u>case</u>.

_____

Common and Proper Nouns

Read the following sentences. Circle the proper noun(s) in each sentence and then write what it names on the line. The first one has been done for you.

1 I buy the *Texas Monthly* every month.

magazine

2 We have two dogs, named Archie and Samantha.

_____

3 In the fall, I will attend Nichols Middle School.

_____

4 We are going to read about the Industrial Revolution.

_____

5 Did you have a good time at our Fourth of July picnic this year?

_____

6 I want to join the National Geographic Society.

_____

Complete the chart by filling in each missing common or proper noun. The first one has been done for you.

Common Noun	Proper Noun
magazine	*The New Yorker*
era	_____
_____	Chicago
pet	_____
president	_____
_____	Memorial Day
_____	Best Toy, Inc.

Common and Proper Nouns

Decide if there is an error in the underlined nouns.
Fill in the bubble next to the correct answer.

1 I think <u>aunt Anita</u> made tacos.
○ Aunt Anita
○ aunt anita
○ correct as is

2 We take a vacation in <u>Redwood National Park</u> every summer.
○ Redwood National park
○ Redwood national park
○ correct as is

3 I have a doctor's appointment on <u>tuesday, May 9</u>.
○ tuesday, may 9
○ Tuesday, May 9
○ correct as is

4 The <u>civil war</u> period is fascinating.
○ Civil war
○ Civil War
○ correct as is

5 Albert bought take-out food last night from <u>Grandma's good eats</u>.
○ Grandma's Good Eats
○ grandma's Good Eats
○ correct as is

6 Josie learned <u>French in France</u>.
○ french in France
○ french in france
○ correct as is

7 Large cats can be found in both <u>north and south America</u>.
○ North and South America
○ north and south america
○ correct as is

8 Carla moved to <u>el Paso, Texas</u>.
○ El paso, Texas
○ El Paso, Texas
○ correct as is

9 I'm planning to take a rafting trip down the <u>Colorado river</u> next month.
○ Colorado River
○ colorado river
○ correct as is

10 I read an interesting story in the <u>*Houston Chronicle*</u> the other day.
○ *Houston chronicle*
○ *houston Chronicle*
○ correct as is

Singular and Plural Nouns

Read the sentences below. Circle any singular common nouns in each sentence and underline any plural common nouns.

A **singular noun** names one person, place, animal, thing, or idea. A **plural noun** names more than one person, place, animal, thing, or idea. A plural noun is most often formed by adding *-s* to the singular. Some nouns add *-es* to form the plural.

1 He loved walking in the park, taking pictures.

2 He had taken several photographs with his camera when he stopped to rest on a bench.

3 A rabbit scurried through the bushes, and several birds sang in the branches above his head.

4 Then, suddenly, two strangers came down the path and headed toward him.

5 As they ran past, they dropped some notes near his right foot.

6 He picked them up and saw that the paper was in code.

7 "I guess this is another case for the members of our agency," he said.

. . . .

Rewrite each sentence using the plural form of the underlined nouns.

1 Ricardo snapped on the <u>light</u> and studied the coded <u>message</u>.

_____

2 Vikki gave him the <u>snapshot</u> of the <u>suspect</u>.

_____

3 He was carrying his <u>newspaper</u> and his <u>suitcase</u>.

_____

Singular and Plural Nouns

Underline the singular noun in each sentence.

1 My brothers and parents decided to take a scenic ride.

2 They chose a winding route that went over the mountains.

3 Of all the things they saw, a deserted mining town was the best.

4 They also saw two foxes standing near the pine tree.

5 Later, the moon made the hills and valleys glow.

6 After it was all over, the boys said, "That was a fantastic trip! Let's go again soon."

. . . .

Underline the plural noun in each sentence.

1 Two sixth-grade classes are touring our city.

2 It's amazing how interesting some of the buildings are.

3 Last week, we visited two old libraries.

4 We also saw a temple, a mosque, and two churches.

5 We also discovered a fancy iron fence and beautiful iron benches.

6 Are other cities as amazing as our city?

 On another sheet of paper, write a brief description of some sights in your hometown. Make sure to include singular and plural nouns to describe people, places, and things.

Singular and Plural Nouns

**Decide if there is an error in the underlined nouns.
Fill in the bubble next to the correct answer.**

1 Deirdre took a trip to several <u>city</u> on the East Coast last summer.
- ○ cities
- ○ citys
- ○ correct as is

2 Rudy saves spare change like <u>pennies</u>.
- ○ penny
- ○ pennys
- ○ correct as is

3 Annie bought two biscuit <u>mixs</u> when she went to the store.
- ○ mixes
- ○ mix
- ○ correct as is

4 We looked for different kinds of <u>shelles</u> as we walked along the beach.
- ○ shell
- ○ shells
- ○ correct as is

5 Quite a few <u>classes</u> in our school went on a field trip yesterday.
- ○ class
- ○ classess
- ○ correct as is

6 Brian bought <u>supply</u> for his trip.
- ○ supplys
- ○ supplies
- ○ correct as is

7 Miko saw a lark hopping among the <u>branchs</u> of a willow tree.
- ○ branches
- ○ branch
- ○ correct as is

8 All the <u>birds</u> scattered when Enrico jogged past a small bush.
- ○ birdes
- ○ bird
- ○ correct as is

9 She made two <u>wishs</u> before blowing out the candles on her birthday cake.
- ○ wishes
- ○ wish
- ○ correct as is

10 We have a few <u>holidays</u> this month when school will not be in session.
- ○ holiday
- ○ holidayes
- ○ correct as is

Possessive Nouns

Underline the possessive noun in each sentence. On the line following each sentence, write *S* if the possessive noun is singular and *P* if it is plural.

> **Possessive nouns** show ownership. To form the possessive of a singular noun, add *'s* (boy's). To form the possessive of a plural noun ending in *-s*, add an apostrophe (girls'). To form the possessive of a plural noun that does not end in *-s*, add *'s* (men's).

1. Earhart's record flight across the Atlantic occurred in 1932. _____

2. During the Atlantic crossing, ice formed on the plane's wings. _____

3. Mexico's president greeted Earhart when she completed another flight from California to Mexico City. _____

4. Amelia Earhart was always interested in women's roles in aviation. _____

5. Men's career choices in aviation were more numerous at the time. _____

6. A university's financial support helped Earhart realize her dream of attempting a flight around the world. _____

· ·

Complete each sentence below using the possessive form of the noun in parentheses ( ).

1. The _____ runway was closed because of the storm. (airport)

2. We could see several _____ nests in the trees as our plane came in for a landing. (bird)

3. The _____ crew had to make quite a few preparations before the flight. (plane)

4. The two _____ attempts to land the planes were successful. (pilot)

5. The _____ luggage was collected by the ground crew and placed on a cart. (man)

6. The _____ coats were stored in an overhead bin on the airplane. (student)

Possessive Nouns

Underline the possessive noun in each sentence. On the line next to each sentence, write the word that names what the possessive noun owns.

1 Greenwood Elementary School's physical education program has been very successful during the past year.

_____

2 The physical education teacher's records show that the students have excelled in many areas.

_____

3 Many students were excited about Ms. Rubowski's plans for physical education at Greenwood.

_____

4 The teacher was ensuring that the Greenwood students met their state's physical fitness standards.

_____

5 We're supposed to do 20 sit-ups by year's end.

_____

6 John Davis's record for push-ups beat the previous record by four.

_____

7 Yesterday, Lisa's speed in a race earned her a blue ribbon.

_____

8 The students' overall performance ranked fifth in the state.

_____

On the line, write the possessive form of each proper noun.

1 Chicago

_____

2 Statue of Liberty

_____

3 Yellowstone National Park

_____

4 St. Louis

_____

5 South Dakota

_____

Possessive Nouns

Read each sentence. Then, fill in the bubble next to the correct possessive form.

1 The ten explorer's equipment had been carefully selected and packed.
- ○ explorers
- ○ explorers'
- ○ correct as is

2 The journeys destination was the North Pole.
- ○ journey's
- ○ journeys'
- ○ correct as is

3 Two boats sailed through the region's icy water.
- ○ regions'
- ○ regions
- ○ correct as is

4 The two boats's designs enabled them to plow through thick ice floes.
- ○ boat's
- ○ boats'
- ○ correct as is

5 The explorers took photos for the Arctic Institutes's study group.
- ○ Arctic Institutes
- ○ Arctic Institute's
- ○ correct as is

6 A storms winds forced them to stop.
- ○ storm's
- ○ storms's
- ○ correct as is

7 The leader of the expedition began to worry about the groups food supply.
- ○ groups'
- ○ group's
- ○ correct as is

8 The next days' calm weather made everyone more confident.
- ○ day's
- ○ days's
- ○ correct as is

9 The womens' cabins were packed with flashlights and radios.
- ○ womens's
- ○ women's
- ○ correct as is

10 Dr. Lewis's journal detailed the progress of the expedition.
- ○ Dr. Lewis'
- ○ Dr. Lewi's
- ○ correct as is

Verb Tenses

The verbs in the following sentences are underlined. Read each sentence. Then, write the tense *(past, present, future)* of each verb on the line.

The **tense** of a verb shows the time of the action. The **present tense** shows action that is happening now. The **past tense** shows action that happened in the past. The **future tense** shows action that will happen in the future.

1 The family <u>arrived</u> in San Francisco.

_____

2 The boat <u>stopped</u> there.

_____

3 Soon, the family <u>will drive</u> across the country.

_____

4 They <u>travel</u> for several days.

_____

5 The author's father <u>crosses</u> an old bridge.

_____

6 The car practically <u>raced</u> across the bridge.

_____

7 This action <u>scared</u> both mother and daughter.

_____

8 They <u>will remember</u> it forever!

_____

9 They <u>will hope</u> for no more similar events.

_____

10 The family <u>settled</u> in an overnight cabin.

_____

11 Jean and her mother <u>step</u> out of the car.

_____

12 They <u>see</u> so many new places.

_____

13 They <u>enjoyed</u> their stop in the Ozark Mountains.

_____

14 Jean <u>will reach</u> her grandparents' house soon.

_____

15 Everyone <u>greets</u> the family there.

_____

 On another sheet of paper, write a paragraph that describes how you felt about your home in the past, how you feel about it right now, and how you will probably regard it in the future.

Verb Tenses

Underline each verb. Write whether it is *present*, *past*, or *future*.

1 My friend Miles stopped by my house. _____

2 He is a serious computer whiz. _____

3 We chatted with some of our classmates on the Internet. _____

4 We also downloaded the lyrics to our favorite song. _____

5 I study the unusual rhymes in the lyrics. _____

6 Someday, I will write great songs like that, too. _____

7 Later in the afternoon, we finished our homework together. _____

8 Tomorrow, we will attend a concert. _____

Write each of the verbs from above in the correct column below. Then, fill in the chart with the other tenses of that verb. The first one is done for you.

Present Tense	Past Tense	Future Tense
1. stop	stopped	will stop
2.		
3.		
4.		
5.		
6.		
7.		
8.		

Verb Tenses

Fill in the bubble that correctly identifies the tense of the underlined word or words.

1 My brother and I <u>explored</u> our new neighborhood today.
○ present
○ past
○ future

2 I really <u>like</u> the bicycle path along the main street.
○ present
○ past
○ future

3 We <u>asked</u> some kids about basketball courts in the area.
○ present
○ past
○ future

4 There <u>is</u> a nearby park with a swimming pool and basketball courts.
○ present
○ past
○ future

5 We <u>will spend</u> a lot of time there!
○ present
○ past
○ future

Fill in the bubble beside the verb that completes each sentence correctly.

1 I _____ the bus trip we took a week ago.
○ enjoy
○ will enjoy
○ enjoyed

2 My family and I _____ the Baseball Hall of Fame last weekend.
○ visit
○ visited
○ will visit

3 Last Saturday, we _____ a lot of new information about baseball.
○ learn
○ learned
○ will learn

4 In the years ahead, many new players _____ members of the Hall of Fame.
○ becomes
○ become
○ will become

5 Tomorrow, I _____ my friend Pat to tell her about this fantastic trip.
○ will call
○ called
○ call

Linking Verbs

> A **linking verb** shows a state of being rather than an action. It links, or connects, the subject of a sentence with a word or words in the predicate.

Underline the verb in each sentence below. Then, draw an arrow between the two words that the verb connects. The first one has been done for you.

1 The dog <u>seemed</u> upset by the storm.

2 Marcia's new kitten feels fluffy.

3 The cake in the bakery window looks delicious.

4 Ray's new CD player sounds terrific.

5 Sarah appeared relieved after the test.

Complete each sentence. Use one of the verbs from the sentences in the above activity. Use each verb only once. The first one has been done for you.

1 After riding his bike all day, Marty _____appeared_____ tired.

2 That new movie I heard about last week _____ terrific.

3 Joanne _____ nervous just before the race.

4 Arthur _____ great in his new suit.

5 The new spring grass _____ soft under my feet.

Complete each sentence with a linking verb and a word that describes the subject.

1 John _____ _____ with his performance on the test.

2 The lamb's woolly coat _____ _____ .

3 The new skyscraper downtown _____ _____ .

Linking Verbs

am	was	look	taste	are	were
feel	smell	is	will	sound	seem

Read each sentence. Underline each linking verb.
Then, draw an arrow between the two words that it connects.

Example   This adventure <u>was</u> risky.

1 I am curious about Ernest Shackleton.

2 His life sounds interesting.

3 Shackleton's Antarctic adventure was dangerous.

4 Still, the men seemed cheerful through it all.

5 The photographs are fascinating.

6 You almost feel the bitter cold.

7 Here are some facts I learned.

8 Seal meat tastes oily.

9 The sea smells salty.

10 Antarctica looks lonely.

Linking Verbs

Fill in the bubble next to the linking verb that is in each sentence.

1 The soda in the refrigerator is very cold.
○ is
○ in
○ very

2 Rose seems confident on the pitcher's mound.
○ confident
○ Rose
○ seems

3 The air feels warm this beautiful spring morning.
○ this
○ warm
○ feels

4 The violent storm appears to be over now.
○ appears
○ storm
○ over

5 Stuart was bored and restless during the long movie.
○ restless
○ was
○ during

Fill in the bubble next to the linking verb that correctly completes each sentence.

1 There _____ a concert in the park tomorrow afternoon.
○ will be
○ was
○ has been

2 I _____ certain that the mayor will attend our play.
○ are
○ am
○ were

3 The thunderstorm _____ very loud last night.
○ will be
○ is
○ was

4 That exhibit _____ postponed.
○ has been
○ were
○ had

5 The batter at the plate _____ eager to score a run.
○ were
○ seems
○ am

Main and Helping Verbs

In each sentence, underline the main verb twice and the helping verb once.

A **main verb** shows the action or state of being in a sentence. A helping verb such as *am, are, has, have, had,* or *will* works with the main verb to show when the action or state of being occurs.

1 I am studying the amazing life of Wilma Rudolph.

2 My class will write reports about this sports legend.

3 We have read an exciting account of her triumphs.

4 Teresa is painting a picture of the famous runner.

5 Matthew and I are working on a poster about Wilma's victories.

6 Wilma had overcome serious physical problems.

7 Her mother had given her a great deal of support.

8 The people in Wilma's hometown were cheering for her.

9 People will remember Wilma Rudolph's accomplishments for many years.

10 Her story has inspired young athletes around the world.

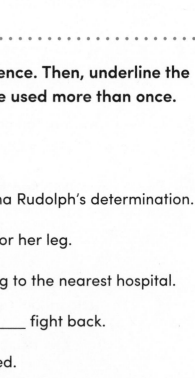

Use one of the helping verbs below to complete each sentence. Then, underline the main verb in each sentence twice. One helping verb will be used more than once.

| am | are | is | will |

1 I _____ reading a book about Wilma Rudolph's determination.

2 Wilma _____ practicing exercises for her leg.

3 She and her mother _____ traveling to the nearest hospital.

4 In spite of the difficulties, Wilma _____ fight back.

5 I _____ rooting for Wilma to succeed.

Main and Helping Verbs

Read the sentences below. Underline the main verbs and write the helping verbs on the lines provided.

1 Wilma had weighed only four pounds at birth.

_____

2 Others have expected little from her.

_____

3 She is becoming a great athlete.

_____

4 Not a single problem has stopped her.

_____

5 People are noticing her skill in basketball.

_____

6 Wilma will surprise everyone.

_____

7 They are urging her to run races.

_____

8 The sweat is flying off her face.

_____

9 She has lunged across the finish line.

_____

10 She is not thinking about her fear or pain.

_____

11 She was forgetting all her problems.

_____

12 People in the crowd were cheering for her.

_____

13 No American woman had captured three
gold medals at one Olympics.

_____

14 She has changed sports history.

_____

Imagine that you were at the Olympics on the day that Wilma Rudolph won three gold medals. On another sheet of paper, write a paragraph describing the reaction of the crowd. What were people doing, thinking, and feeling? Use main and helping verbs in your writing.

Main and Helping Verbs

Fill in the bubble next to the helping verb that correctly completes each sentence.

1 Lily, Frank, and I _____ joining a neighborhood swimming team.
- ○ am
- ○ is
- ○ are

2 I _____ thought about joining the team for a couple of months.
- ○ was
- ○ had
- ○ has

3 Frank _____ taken diving lessons at a YMCA indoor pool.
- ○ has
- ○ have
- ○ is

4 We _____ practiced a great deal.
- ○ will
- ○ has
- ○ have

5 The team's coach _____ analyzing everyone's strengths and weaknesses.
- ○ is
- ○ are
- ○ have

6 The coach _____ post the results on the bulletin board in two weeks.
- ○ will
- ○ have
- ○ had

7 Our team's season _____ not begun.
- ○ is
- ○ have
- ○ has

8 Our team _____ probably compete with other teams from the area.
- ○ have
- ○ had
- ○ will

9 We _____ going with my mother to a sports equipment store tomorrow.
- ○ was
- ○ are
- ○ is

10 I _____ outgrown the swimsuit I wore last summer.
- ○ have
- ○ was
- ○ will

Irregular Verbs

On the line, write the past-tense or the past-participle form of the verb in parentheses ( ).

An **irregular verb** does not form the past tense or past participle by adding -*ed*. The **past participle** is the form of the verb used with *have, has,* or *had*.

1 I _____ I lost my math book. (think)

2 My friend had _____ a fancy seashell. (find)

3 Ed _____ his new CD to my house. (bring)

4 Have you _____ the new coach? (meet)

5 She _____ she would get the team in shape. (say)

6 My neighbors _____ me for babysitting. (pay)

7 John _____ the football. (catch)

8 The little boy _____ his balloon tightly. (hold)

9 I have _____ about learning a new sport. (think)

10 The first night, I _____ the new puppy in my room. (keep)

11 Denise _____ a gold locket in the park the other day. (find)

12 We have already _____ for our tickets. (pay)

Use each of the following verbs in a sentence.

write	wrote	have written

1 _____

2 _____

3 _____

Irregular Verbs

Read each sentence. On the line, write the past-tense or past-participle form of the verb in parentheses ( ).

1 They had _____ home to America. (came)

2 They _____ about their trip across the ocean. (speak)

3 They _____ many things to do. (find)

4 They _____ and danced on the ship. (sing)

5 They _____ pictures, too. (take)

6 Jean Fritz has _____ about the journey. (write)

7 She has _____ some good moments to retell. (chose)

8 Some events are _____ in her memory. (freeze)

9 Time has not _____ them from her. (steal)

10 She _____ her first sight of America very exciting. (find)

11 She _____ a glimpse of the Hawaiian Islands. (catch)

12 She has never _____ sight of them in her mind. (lose)

13 Lines of poetry _____ from her lips. (spring)

14 Many people have _____ this is an interesting story. (say)

15 Jean Fritz has _____ a reputation as a good author. (build)

 On another sheet of paper, write about an exciting adventure in your own past. Use at least one past-tense form and one past-participle form.

Irregular Verbs

Choose the verb form that correctly completes each sentence.
Fill in the bubble next to your answer.

1 My friend Alex _____ several
National Parks.
○ see
○ has saw
○ has seen

2 He _____ an arrowhead in Montana.
○ find
○ has find
○ found

3 In Colorado, he _____ a real dinosaur
fossil in his hand.
○ held
○ hold
○ has hold

4 He _____ a visit to Abraham Lincoln's
birthplace in Kentucky.
○ pay
○ paid
○ has pay

5 He was on Assateague Island when
wild ponies _____ ashore.
○ swims
○ swam
○ has swum

6 I _____ him that next time I would
go with him.
○ tells
○ has told
○ told

7 Once, I _____ home shells from
the ocean.
○ brings
○ has bring
○ brought

8 I _____ many souvenirs from the trips
I have taken.
○ have kept
○ has kept
○ keeps

9 Where were you when the bell _____?
○ ring
○ rang
○ rings

10 Oh, no, I _____ my souvenir!
○ has broke
○ have broken
○ breaks

Pronouns

Underline the pronoun in each sentence. Then, circle the word or words to which the pronoun refers.

> A **pronoun** is a word that takes the place of a noun or nouns. Pronouns show number. They indicate one or more than one.

1 Savannah and Elana agreed to eat lunch together. They decided to meet at noon.

2 "Which train should I take?" David wondered, studying the train schedule.

3 Melanie opened the door. She was surprised when people shouted, "Happy birthday!"

4 The barn might look deserted, but it has become a home to many birds.

5 Frank has already eaten half of the bread he baked this afternoon.

· ·

Read each sentence pair. Underline the pronouns. On the lines, write the pronouns and the nouns they replace. The first one has been done for you.

1 Joe bought a gift last week. He gave it to Margarita yesterday.

He = Joe _____ it = gift _____

2 Many people are in line, waiting to buy this book. They have been waiting to buy it all afternoon.

_____ _____

3 Amy and Duncan paddled the canoe upriver for three hours. "We have been paddling all afternoon," said Amy, "and I am getting tired."

_____ _____

4 Did Emma get the eggs? She will need them for dinner.

_____ _____

Pronouns

Read the sentences. Write a pronoun on the line that could take the place of the underlined words.

1 <u>Talent shows</u> can make people nervous. _____

2 <u>A talent show</u> gives people a chance to show off. _____

3 <u>My younger brother</u> was in the talent show at my school. _____

4 Lots of people clapped loudly for <u>my brother</u>. _____

5 <u>My older sister</u> did not want to be in the show. _____

6 I did not blame <u>my older sister</u>. _____

7 I was nervous about being in <u>the talent show</u>, too. _____

8 <u>Pam, Alicia, and I</u> decided to sing a round. _____

9 People clapped politely for <u>Pam, Alicia, and me</u>. _____

10 We thanked <u>the audience members</u> for applauding. _____

11 You can ask <u>Ms. Renko</u> about how well we did! _____

12 Now <u>my sister</u> is thinking about being in a show. _____

13 I asked <u>my parents</u> if my brother, sister, and I could practice at home. _____

14 Next year, <u>the talent show</u> will be even better! _____

Imagine that you are dancing or singing in a talent show and the music suddenly stops or begins to skip. On another sheet of paper, write two or three sentences telling how you feel and how others react. Underline all the pronouns that you use.

Pronouns

Fill in the bubble next to the pronoun that correctly replaces the underlined words in each sentence.

1. Lou picked some flowers in the garden and put <u>the flowers</u> in a vase.
   - ○ it
   - ○ them
   - ○ her

2. Don't buy those shoes if <u>the shoes</u> don't feel comfortable.
   - ○ it
   - ○ I
   - ○ they

3. Sarah said <u>Sarah</u> would help wash the car today.
   - ○ I
   - ○ we
   - ○ she

4. Mel made a surprise dinner for <u>Laura</u>.
   - ○ her
   - ○ him
   - ○ them

5. Will played a great game, and everyone patted <u>Will</u> on the back.
   - ○ them
   - ○ him
   - ○ us

Fill in the bubble next to the pronoun that correctly completes each sentence.

1. Cindy, Jon, and I decided that _____ would all meet after school.
   - ○ we
   - ○ he
   - ○ she

2. The ball flew overhead, and then _____ disappeared into the trees.
   - ○ it
   - ○ they
   - ○ we

3. Leo told all nine of _____ the news.
   - ○ me
   - ○ him
   - ○ us

4. I thanked my parents for the present they gave _____.
   - ○ it
   - ○ me
   - ○ them

5. The coach said, " _____ am sure we'll win!"
   - ○ we
   - ○ I
   - ○ me

Subject and Object Pronouns

A **subject pronoun** indicates who or what performs the action of a sentence. *I, you, he, she, it, we,* and *they* are subject pronouns. An **object pronoun** indicates who or what receives the action. *Me, you, him, her, it, us,* and *them* are object pronouns.

Read the sentence pairs below. Underline the pronoun in the second sentence. Then, circle the noun it replaces in the first sentence.

1. The woodcutter saw a neighbor working in the garden. The woodcutter approached him.

2. "Those roses are beautiful," said the woodcutter. "They have a wonderful scent."

3. "This garden is a joy," said the woodcutter's neighbor. "It gets a lot of sun."

4. "There's an easier way to dig holes," said the woodcutter. "A shovel could dig them in half the time."

5. The neighbor just smiled at the woodcutter and said, "Good day to you, sir."

6. The woodcutter shrugged. Then, he walked away.

· ·

Underline all pronouns in each sentence below. Then, above each one, write *S* if it is a subject pronoun, or *O* if it is an object pronoun.

1. The woodcutter's wife asked him to go to the woods.

2. "I want you to chop some wood," she said.

3. "We have guests coming to visit us," said the woodcutter's wife.

4. "They will be here soon. Let's serve them dinner," his wife continued.

5. The woodcutter found an ax, and he picked it up.

6. "I will be back in a jiffy," the woodcutter told her.

7. "I will be here," the wife answered. "Don't make me wait too long."

Subject and Object Pronouns

In each sentence, circle the correct pronoun in parentheses ( ).

1 The woodcutter's wife warns (he, him).

2 The woodcutter does not hear (she, her).

3 The woodcutter and (she, her) often ignore each other.

4 (They, Them) do not see eye to eye.

5 The woodcutter just watched (them, they).

6 Amy and (I, me) felt sorry for the woodcutter.

7 (Us, We) might have done the same thing.

8 (He, Him) did not seem like such an unlikable character.

9 We told Katie and (she, her) about this story.

10 (They, Them) had different ideas about the story.

11 Matt wanted Katie and (I, me) to agree with him.

12 We asked (he, him) to explain his ideas.

13 Then, he told Katie and (I, me) his opinion.

14 The opinions were different. We couldn't change (they, them)!

15 (He, him), Katie, and I will have to read it again.

 Why don't some people listen to good advice? On another sheet of paper, write two or three sentences explaining why this might be so. Use as many subject and object pronouns as possible.

Subject and Object Pronouns

Fill in the bubble next to the pronoun that correctly completes each sentence.

1 _____will all meet at my house after the game.
- ○ We
- ○ Them
- ○ Us

2 _____ decided to hold a meeting tomorrow after school.
- ○ Us
- ○ Them
- ○ They

3 Lydia and _____ are going to be in the play.
- ○ me
- ○ I
- ○ us

4 Bruce met _____ at the football game.
- ○ we
- ○ I
- ○ me

5 Jeff bought a used bike and painted _____ red.
- ○ it
- ○ him
- ○ them

Decide if the underlined part of each sentence is correct. Fill in the bubble next to the right answer.

1 <u>They</u> tried out for the basketball team.
- ○ Them
- ○ Us
- ○ correct as is

2 Susan promised to take <u>they</u> to the lake tomorrow.
- ○ them
- ○ we
- ○ correct as is

3 Dad took <u>I and Mark</u> to the beach today.
- ○ Mark and I
- ○ Mark and me
- ○ correct as is

4 <u>Her and me</u> have been friends for a long time.
- ○ Me and she
- ○ She and I
- ○ correct as is

5 <u>Me and him</u> are exactly the same age.
- ○ He and I
- ○ Him and me
- ○ correct as is

Possessive Pronouns

**Circle the possessive pronoun in each sentence.
Then, draw an arrow to the noun that it describes.**

A **possessive pronoun** shows ownership. You can use a possessive pronoun to replace a possessive noun. The possessive pronouns *my, your, his, her, its, our,* and *their* come before nouns. *Mine, yours, hers, his, ours,* and *theirs* are used alone. *His* can be used before a noun or alone.

1 My family is moving next summer, so we're cleaning out the house.

2 You wouldn't believe what we found in our attic!

3 Mom and Dad discovered a stack of old photos from their honeymoon.

4 Ella found her first bicycle.

5 Adam found his diary from third grade.

6 Now he is looking for its key.

7 What do you think you would find in your house?

Write the possessive pronoun that goes with each subject pronoun.

1 I _____

2 you _____

3 he _____

4 she _____

5 it _____

6 we _____

7 they _____

**Choose two pairs of pronouns from the list above.
Then, write a sentence using each pair.**

1 _____

2 _____

Possessive Pronouns

**Circle the pronoun in parentheses ( )
that correctly completes each sentence.**

> **Possessive pronouns** show ownership. You can use a possessive pronoun to replace a possessive noun. The pronouns *my, your, his, her, its, our,* and *their* come before nouns. The pronouns *mine, yours, his, hers, ours,* and *theirs* stand alone.

1 They practiced (their, theirs) lines over and over again.

2 She uses (her, hers) talent to create beautiful heroines.

3 "Is that (my, mine) playbook?" asked Lily.

4 "No! It is (my, mine)," replied Sean.

5 The play is about a woman's struggle to find (her, hers) missing sister.

. . . .

Rewrite the sentences, using possessive pronouns in place of the underlined words.

1 Which dresses in the closet are <u>Barbara's</u>?

_____

2 This is <u>Ken and Tony's</u> collection of dried flowers.

_____

3 I am enjoying <u>Paul's</u> book.

_____

4 <u>Elizabeth's</u> disappointment showed clearly.

_____

5 Is this <u>Kevin's</u> idea of a joke?

_____

Look through a magazine article. Underline all the possessive pronouns you find.

Possessive Pronouns

Fill in the bubble next to the pronoun that correctly completes each sentence.

1 Every night, the older children on _____ block get together.
- ○ mine
- ○ my
- ○ ours

2 If Lila is there, we play basketball at _____ house.
- ○ her
- ○ hers
- ○ its

3 When Ray and Maria are home, we play at _____.
- ○ its
- ○ theirs
- ○ their

4 Tonight, Al and Rob are bringing _____ soccer ball.
- ○ his
- ○ theirs
- ○ their

5 Tomorrow night, I will bring _____.
- ○ mine
- ○ my
- ○ our

Decide which pronoun correctly replaces the underlined words. Fill in the bubble next to your answer.

1 <u>Mr. and Mrs. Espy's</u> daughter Tracy won a trophy for soccer.
- ○ Theirs
- ○ Their
- ○ Her

2 "This Year's Most Valuable Player" is written on the <u>trophy's</u> base.
- ○ my
- ○ its
- ○ her

3 <u>Tracy's</u> team will play in the State Championship.
- ○ Our
- ○ Her
- ○ Hers

4 Last year, <u>Alan's</u> school won the championship.
- ○ him
- ○ his
- ○ its

5 This year, victory will be <u>Tracy's</u>.
- ○ her
- ○ theirs
- ○ hers

ANSWER KEY

Page 5
1. (This story) tells about Jamie and Gramma Bowman. 2. (Gramma Bowman) used to tell Jamie stories. 3. (Jamie's great-grandmother) loved to see the fox's tracks. 4. (Her best friend Pippin the Fox,) left the tracks. 5. (That clever fox) delighted Gramma. 6. (Gramma's song) is a kind of fox song.
1. The autumn <u>leaves</u> 2. The old <u>man</u> 3. The fall <u>season</u> 4. The <u>leaves</u> 5. The cold, autumn <u>wind</u> 6. Gramma Bowman, a wise <u>woman</u> 7. The old <u>leaves</u> 8. Their final <u>dances</u> 9. The very best <u>dances</u> 10. Gramma Bowman's <u>story</u>

Page 6
1. Old, wise <u>Gramma Bowman</u> 2. The first <u>line</u> of the song 3. The <u>words</u> of the song 4. This <u>song</u>, a kind of chant 5. Her <u>dream</u> 6. A <u>fox</u> with glistening eyes 7. The <u>fox</u>, a mysterious animal
1. <u>events</u> 2. <u>conversations</u> 3. <u>actions</u> 4. <u>Jamie</u> 5. <u>characters</u> 6. <u>lessons</u> 7. <u>Gramma Bowman</u> 8. <u>nature</u>

Page 7
1. Jamie's great-grandmother 2. This amazing woman 3. Their house on the Winooski River 4. The woods up the hill 5. Sweet, wild blueberries
1. settlers 2. Blueberries 3. bushes 4. plants 5. care

Page 8
Action: 1. <u>listen</u> to the radio. 3. <u>danced</u> in the gym last Friday afternoon. 4. <u>sang</u> some "oldies." 6. <u>stood</u> along the side of the gym.
State-of-being: 2. <u>like</u> the latest pop music. 5. <u>was</u> a huge success among students and teachers. 7. <u>seemed</u> amused by the music and dancing.
Answers will vary.

Page 9
1. <u>would start soon.</u> 2. <u>was running out to the field beside Ken.</u> 3. <u>ran down Ken Jr.'s back.</u> 4. <u>was none other than his dad.</u> 5. <u>let out a roar.</u> 6. <u>knew this was a great moment.</u> 7. <u>felt so happy!</u>
1. <u>read</u> 2. <u>are</u> 3. <u>played</u> 4. <u>were</u> 5. <u>made</u> 6. <u>sent</u> 7. <u>appeared</u> 8. <u>remain</u>

Page 10
1. performed a musical Friday 2. attended the event, too 3. was the musical director 4. chose the musical numbers 5. worked behind the scenes

1. were 2. collected 3. is 4. was 5. congratulated

Page 11
1. <u>Families</u> (and) <u>friends</u> 2. <u>leave</u> their homes (and) <u>lose</u> 3. <u>Intelligence</u>, <u>courage</u>, (and) <u>luck</u> 4. <u>Food</u> (and) clean <u>water</u> 5. <u>join</u> the army (or) <u>work</u>
1. Annemarie and Ellen played with the dolls. 2. Kirsti cried and complained about the shoes. 3. Annemarie brushed her hair and handed the brush to Ellen. 4. Families hid in the house or fled to the forest.

Page 12
1. <u>Annemarie</u> (and) <u>Ellen</u> 2. <u>homes</u> (and) <u>families</u> 3. <u>talk</u> (or) <u>giggle</u> 4. <u>joke</u>, <u>laugh</u>, (and) <u>play</u> 5. <u>Rosens</u> (or) the <u>Johansens</u> 6. <u>Families</u> (and) <u>friends</u> 7. <u>hide</u> Ellen (and) <u>keep</u> 8. <u>reads</u> (and) <u>sings</u> 9. <u>Denmark</u>, <u>Holland</u>, (and) other <u>countries</u> 10. <u>succeed</u> (or) <u>fail</u>
Sentences will vary.

Page 13
2, 3, and 10 are correct as is
1. George, Tina, and I 4. hit a ball and lost it 5. Tina and I 6. pointed and showed us 7. looked up, turned, and walked 8. joined us and helped 9. get the custodian or find

Page 14
1. I want to go to the movies, **but** my friend Pat does not. 2. It rained last night, **and** we had to stay home. 3. Ed will drive to Texas, **or** he will take the train. 4. It snowed this morning, **but** the sun came out this afternoon.
1. We wanted to ride our bikes home, but mine had a flat tire. 2. I will finish the job today, or Bob will finish it tomorrow. 3. The whistle blew, and the train pulled out of the station.

Page 15
1. Our cousins arrived, **and** we were very happy to see them. 2. Eileen had cut her hair short, **but** her twin sister, Emily, still had long hair. 3. They had always looked exactly alike, **and** I could not get used to them! 4. Would they play with me, **or** would they only play with my older sisters? 5. First, Eileen gave me a hug, **and** then Emily did the same.
Paragraphs will vary.

Page 16
2, 5, and 8 are correct as is
1. weekend, and I 3. bookshelf, but I 4. neighbor, but most 6. store, but we 7. there, but no one 9. empty, but the library books 10. books, but my interest

Page 17
1. <u>Mr. Sherlock Holmes</u>, <u>detective</u> 2. <u>character</u>, <u>Sir Arthur Conan Doyle</u> 3. <u>Holmes</u>, <u>stories</u>, <u>novels</u>, <u>Doyle</u>, *The Sign of Four* 4. <u>friend</u>, <u>Dr. John Watson</u> 5. <u>mysteries</u>, <u>city</u>, <u>London</u>
1. proper, common, proper 2. proper, common 3. common, proper 4. common, common, common 5. proper, proper, common

Page 18
1. (Texas Monthly), magazine 2. (Archie) and (Samantha), pet names 3. (Nichols Middle School), school 4. (Industrial Revolution), historical era 5. (Fourth of July), holiday 6. (National Geographic Society), organization
Possible answers shown.
Common noun: city, holiday, business
Proper noun: Ice Age, Rover, George Washington

Page 19
2, 6, and 10 are correct as is
1. Aunt Anita 3. Tuesday, May 9 4. Civil War 5. Grandma's Good Eats 7. North and South America 8. El Paso, Texas 9. Colorado River

Page 20
1. (park), pictures 2. photographs, (camera), (bench) 3. (rabbit), bushes, birds, branches, (head) 4. strangers, (path) 5. notes, (foot) 6. (paper), (code) 7. (case), members, (agency)
1. Ricardo snapped on the lights and studied the coded messages. 2. Vikki gave him the snapshots of the suspects. 3. He was carrying his newspapers and his suitcases.

Page 21
1. ride 2. route 3. town 4. tree 5. moon 6. trip
1. classes 2. buildings 3. libraries 4. churches 5. benches 6. cities

Page 22
2, 5, 8, and 10 are correct as is
1. cities 3. mixes 4. shells 6. supplies 7. branches 9. wishes

Page 23
1. Earhart's, S 2. plane's, S
3. Mexico's, S 4. women's, P
5. Men's, P 6. university's, S
1. airport's 2. birds' 3. plane's
4. pilots' 5. man's 6. students'

Page 24
1. School's, program 2. teacher's,
records 3. Ms. Rubowski's, plans
4. state's, standards 5. year's, end
6. Davis's, record 7. Lisa's, speed
8. students', performance
1. Chicago's 2. Statue of Liberty's
3. Yellowstone National Park's
4. St. Louis's 5. South Dakota's

Page 25
3 and 10 are correct as is
1. explorers' 2. journey's 4. boats'
5. Arctic Institute's 6. storm's 7. group's
8. day's 9. women's

Page 26
1. past 2. past 3. future 4. present
5. present 6. past 7. past 8. future
9. future 10. past 11. present 12. present
13. past 14. future 15. present

Page 27
1. stopped, past 2. is, present
3. chatted, past 4. downloaded, past
5. study, present 6. will write, future
7. finished, past 8. will attend, future
2. is, was, will be 3. chat, chatted, will
chat 4. download, downloaded, will
download 5. study, studied, will study
6. write, wrote, will write 7. finish,
finished, will finish 8. attend, attended,
will attend

Page 28
1. past 2. present 3. past
4. present 5. future
1. enjoyed 2. visited 3. learned
4. will become 5. will call

Page 29
2. kitten feels fluffy
3. cake looks delicious
4. player sounds terrific
5. Sarah appeared relieved
Sample answers: 2. sounds 3. seemed
4. looks 5. feels
Sample answers: 1. was, pleased 2.
feels, soft 3. looks, beautiful

Page 30
1. I am curious
2. life sounds interesting
3. adventure was dangerous
4. men seemed cheerful
5. photographs are fascinating
6. You almost feel the bitter cold
7. Here are some facts
8. meat tastes oily
9. sea smells salty
10. Antarctica looks lonely

Page 31
1. is 2. seems 3. feels
4. appears 5. was
1. will be 2. am 3. was
4. has been 5. seems

Page 32
1. am studying 2. will write 3. have
read 4. is painting 5. are working
6. had overcome 7. had given
8. were cheering 9. will remember
10. has inspired
1. am reading 2. is practicing 3. are
traveling 4. will fight 5. am rooting

Page 33
1. weighed, had 2. expected, have
3. becoming, is 4. stopped, has
5. noticing, are 6. surprise, will
7. urging, are 8. flying, is 9. lunged, has
10. thinking, is 11. forgetting, was
12. cheering, were 13. captured, had
14. changed, has

Page 34
1. are 2. had 3. has 4. have 5. is
6. will 7. has 8. will 9. are 10. have

Page 35
1. thought 2. found 3. brought 4. met
5. said 6. paid 7. caught 8. held
9. thought 10. kept 11. found 12. paid
Sentences will vary.

Page 36
1. come 2. spoke 3. found 4. sang
5. took 6. written 7. chosen 8. frozen
9. stolen 10. found 11. caught 12. lost
13. sprang 14. said 15. built

Page 37
1. has seen 2. found 3. held 4. paid
5. swam 6. told 7. brought 8. have kept
9. rang 10. have broken

Page 38
1. (Savannah and Elana), They
2. I, (David) 3. (Melanie), She
4. (barn), it 5. (Frank), he
2. They, it They = Many people, it = book
3. We, I We = Amy and Duncan, I = Amy
4. She, them She = Emma, them = eggs

Page 39
1. They 2. It 3. He 4. him 5. She
6. her 7. it 8. We 9. us 10. them
11. her 12. she 13. them 14. it

Page 40
1. them 2. they 3. she 4. her 5. him
1. we 2. it 3. us 4. me 5. I

Page 41
1. (neighbor), him 2. (roses), They
3. (garden), It 4. (holes), them
5. (woodcutter), you
6. (woodcutter), he
1. him: O 2. I: S, you: O, she: S
3. We: S, us: O 4. They: S, them: O
5. he: S, it: O 6. I: S, her: O 7. I: S, me: O

Page 42
1. him 2. her 3. she 4. They 5. them
6. I 7. We 8. He 9. her 10. They
11. me 12. him 13. me 14. them 15. He

Page 43
1. We 2. They 3. I 4. me 5. it
1. correct as is 2. them 3. Mark and me
4. She and I 5. He and I

Page 44
1. (My) family
2. (our) attic
3. (their) honeymoon
4. (her) first bicycle
5. (his) diary
6. (its) key
7. (your) house
1. my 2. your 3. his 4. her 5. its
6. our 7. their
Sentences will vary.

Page 45
1. their 2. her 3. my 4. mine 5. her
1. Which dresses in the closet are hers?
2. This is their collection of dried flowers.
3. I am enjoying his book.
4. Her disappointment showed clearly.
5. Is this his idea of a joke?

Page 46
1. my 2. her 3. theirs 4. their 5. mine
1. Their 2. its 3. Her 4. his 5. hers